Cambridge Little Steps 1

Student's Book

Gabriela Zapiain

CAMBRIDGE UNIVERSITY PRESS

Cambridge Little Steps 1

1 What can we see at school?

Listen. Say. Sing.

teacher

boy

girl

school

Key Vocabulary: *teacher, boy, girl, school*

Tracks: 1 and 2

What is the story about?

Listen. Point. Say.

What Can You See?

sun

tree

Key Vocabulary: *teacher, boy, girl, school, sun, tree*

Key Language: *What can you see?*

Track: 3

How does the story help us answer our Big Question?

Listen. Point. Say.

Key Vocabulary: *teacher, boy, girl, school, sun, tree*

Key Language: *What can you see? I can see a (girl).*

Track: 3

Where does the story take place?

Look. Say. Color.

Key Language: *Where does the story take place? In a ...*

Is it important to keep our classroom clean?

Look. Color. Talk.

Key Vocabulary: *children, cleaning*

Key Language: *Keep our classroom clean.*

What can we see in our classroom?

Listen. Say. Trace.

book

crayon

chair

table

Key Vocabulary: *book, chair, crayon, table*

Key Language: *Is it a chair? Yes. / No.*

Track: 4

What is it? Is it a book?

Look. Stick. Listen.

Key Vocabulary: *book, chair, crayon, table*

Key Language: *Is it a (book)? Yes, it is. No, it isn't. What is it? It's a (book).*

Track: 4

Is the classroom door open or closed?

Look. Match. Say.

Key Vocabulary: *open, closed*

Key Language: *The (door) is open / closed.*

Who helps you before school?

Listen. Point. Color.

Key Vocabulary: *Dad, Mom, Mia, Leo, Tickles*

Track: 5

What's your name?

Glue. Say.

Leo

Mia

Key Language: *What's your name? My name is ... What's his / her name? His / her name is ...*

How do you greet people at school?

Trace. Listen. Say.

Key Language: *Hello. Hi! How are you today? I'm fine, thank you. Goodbye, Bye-bye!*

Track: 6

What are the rules in the classroom?

Say. Point. Color.

Listen.

Take turns.

Share.

Key Vocabulary: *classroom rules*

Key Language: *Listen. Take turns. Share.*

How many books can you see?

Say. Trace. Count.

Key Vocabulary: *one*

Key Language: *Show me (one). How many (books) can you see?*

Make. Say.

What can we see at school?

1

2

3

4

Key Vocabulary: *teacher, boy, girl, school, book, chair, table, crayon*

Key Language: *What can you see? I can see a (girl). Is it a (table)? Yes, it is. No, it isn't. It's a (book).*

2 What do we look like?

Listen. Say. Sing.

face

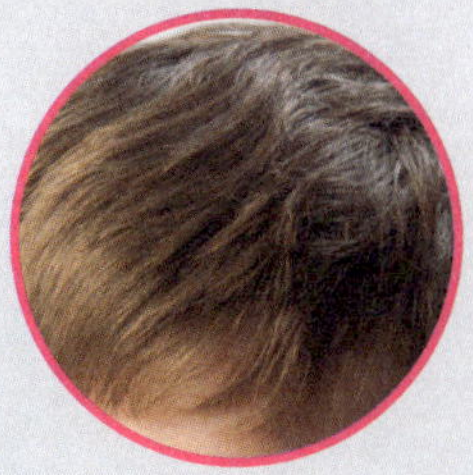

hair

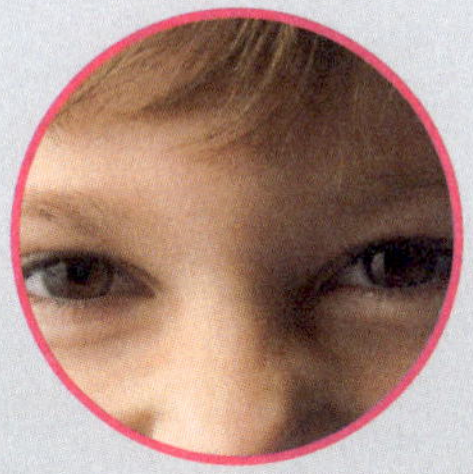

eyes

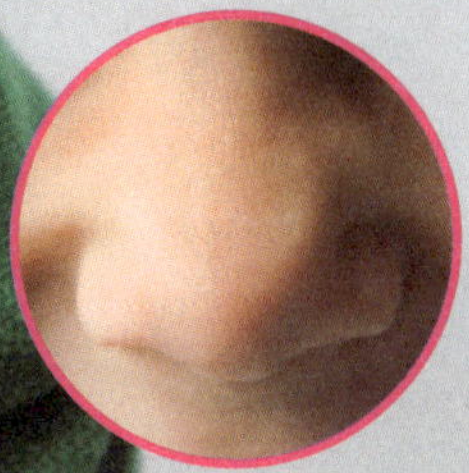

nose

Key Vocabulary: *face, hair, eyes, nose*

Tracks: 7 and 8

What is the story about?

Listen. Point. Say.

Can You Find Me?

hat

kite

mouse

Key Vocabulary: *hair, face, eyes, nose, hat, kite, mouse*

Key Language: *What do you look like? My hair is (brown). My eyes are (green).*

Track: 9

How does the story help us answer our Big Question?

Listen. Point. Say.

Key Language: *Can you find him / her? Where is s/he? His hair is (brown). Her eyes are (blue).*

Track: 9

Who are the characters in the story?

Look. Say. Trace.

Key Vocabulary: *character*

Key Language: *What does s/he look like? She has (brown) hair. He has (green) eyes.*

Is it important to respect differences?

Look. Color. Talk.

Key Language: *They are different. They have the same / different (hair).*

Can you name other parts of your face?

Listen. Say. Color.

forehead

mouth

ears

cheeks

Key Vocabulary: *forehead, mouth, ears, cheeks*

Tracks: 8 and 10

Can you say the chant?

Follow. Trace. Say.

Key Language: *This is my (nose). These are my (eyes).*

Can you find red?

Point. Say. Match.

Key Vocabulary: *red*

Key Language: *The (paint) is red. What color is the (apple)?*

What feelings do the faces show?

Listen. Say. Trace.

How do you feel?

Look. Color. Say.

Key Language: *How do you feel? Are you sad / happy / angry? Yes, I am. No, I'm not. Is s/he (sad)? Yes, s/he is. No, s/he isn't.*

How do you ask people about their feelings?

Color. Listen. Say.

Key Language: *How do you feel? I feel happy / sad / angry.*

Track: 12

What do twins look like?

Look. Say. Trace.

Key Vocabulary: *twins*

Key Language: *They look the same / different. Do they look the same / different?*

How many happy faces can you see?

Say. Count. Match.

2

Key Vocabulary: *one, two*

Key Language: *Show me (two). How many ... can you see?*

Make. Say.

What do we look like?

1

2

3

4

Key Vocabulary: *hair, face, mouth, nose, forehead, eyes, ears, cheeks*

Key Language: *This is my (nose). These are my (eyes). My hair is (brown). My eyes are (blue). I feel happy.*

3 What can our bodies do?

Listen. Say. Sing.

arms

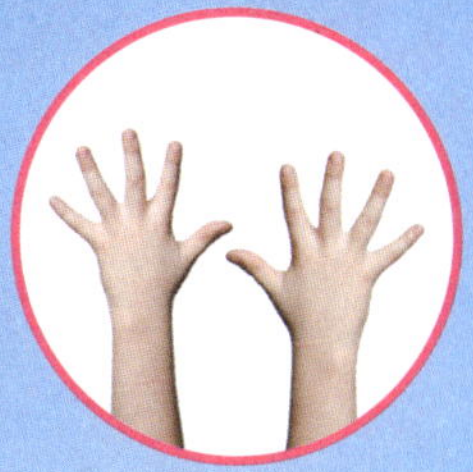

hands

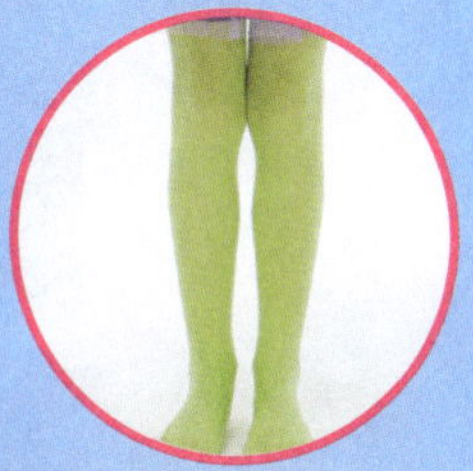

legs

feet

Key Vocabulary: *arms, hands, legs, feet*

Tracks: 13 and 14

What is the story about?

Listen. Point. Say.

The Coconut Band

gorilla

jump

feet

Key Vocabulary: *gorilla, jump, feet, arms, hands, legs*

Key Language: *What can you see? What can s/he do? Can s/he (jump)?*

Track: 15

How does the story help us answer our Big Question?

Listen. Point. Say.

Key Language: *What can you see? What can they do? Can they jump / tap?*

Track: 15

Is this a scene from the story?

Look. Say. Trace.

Key Language: *What can you see? Who are the characters? What can they do? Is this a scene from the story?*

Is it important to wash our hands with soap?

Look. Color. Talk.

Key Vocabulary: *soap, clean, dirty*

Key Language: *Wash your hands. Is it important? Yes. / No.*

Can you name the body parts?

Listen. Stick. Say.

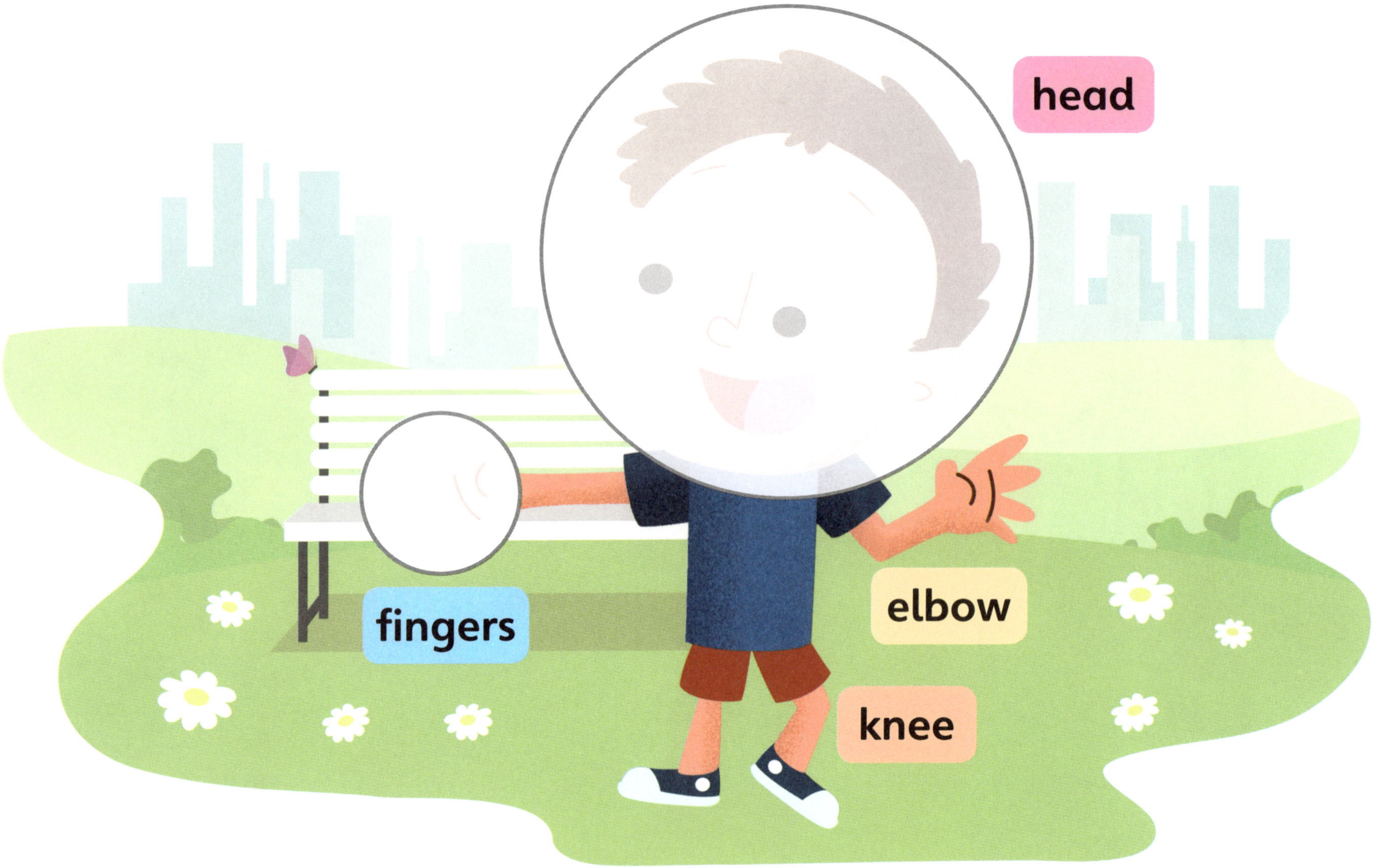

Key Vocabulary: *head, elbow, fingers, knee*

Track: 16

What body parts do you have?

Look. Say. Circle.

Key Language: *I have a (head). I have two (knees). S/he has a (head). S/he has two (feet).*

Which objects are blue?

Look. Match. Say.

Key Vocabulary: *blue*

Key Language: *The (paint) is blue. What color is (it)? Is the (book) blue? Yes. / No. Which objects are blue?*

What are the actions?

Match. Listen. Say.

run

dance

crawl

kick

Key Vocabulary: *run, dance, crawl, kick*

Track: 17

What can the children do?

Look. Say. Color.

Key Language: *Can she (dance)? Yes, s/he can. No, s/he can't. S/he can (crawl). Can you (run)? Yes, I can. No, I can't. I can (kick).*

How do you ask permission?

Listen. Say. Trace.

Key Language: *I wash my hands. May I go to the bathroom? May I wash my hands? Yes, you may.*

Track: 18

Can we make art with our bodies?

Paint. Talk.

Key Language: *What can we do with (our fingers)? We can (paint).*

How many children can you see?

Say. Count. Match.

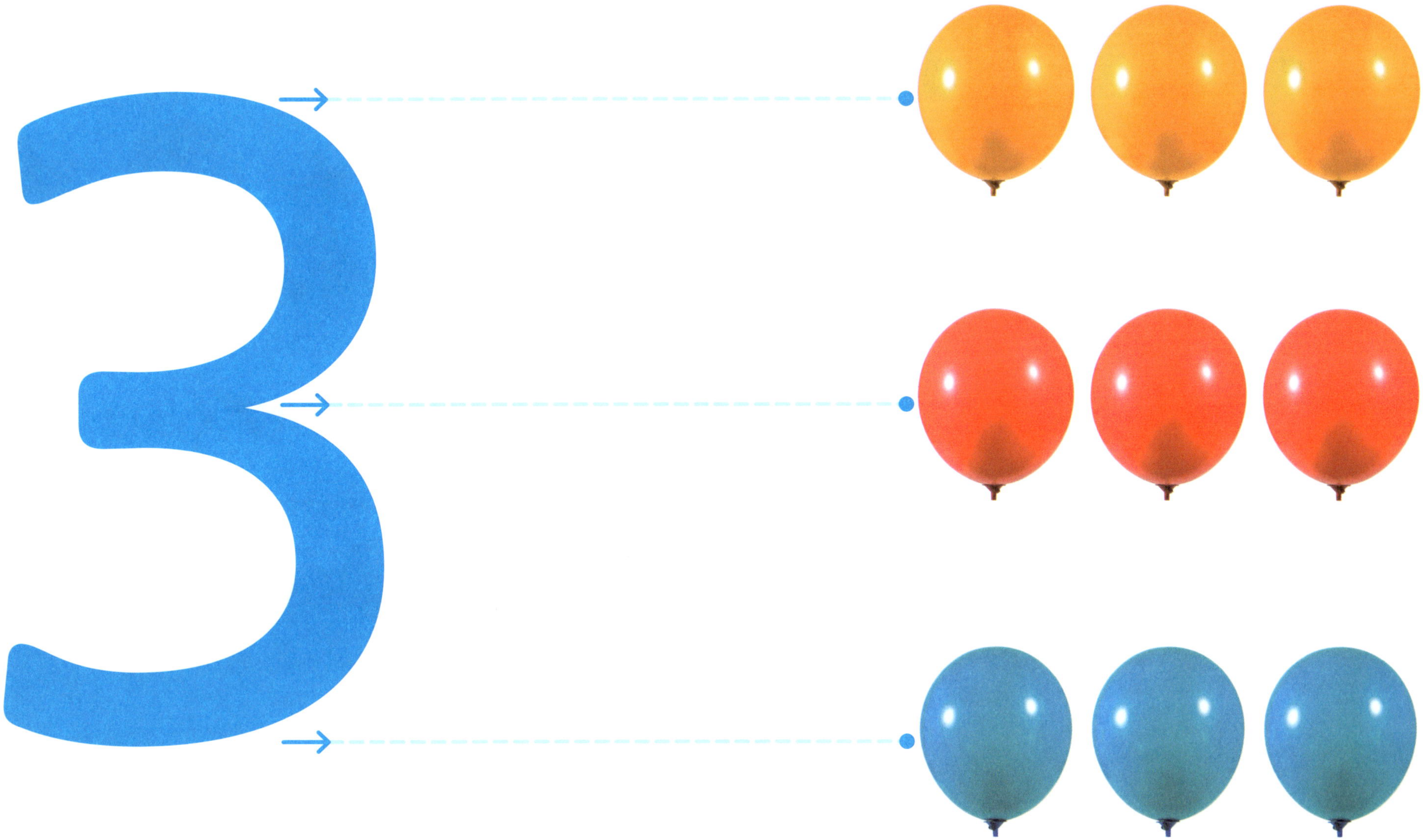

Key Vocabulary: *one, two, three*

Key Language: *Show me (three). How many (balloons) can you see?*

Make. Say.

What can our bodies do?

1

2

3

4

Key Vocabulary: *arms, hands, legs, feet, head, fingers, elbow, knee, run, dance, crawl, kick*

Key Language: *I have two (feet). I can (dance). I have two (legs). I can (kick).*

4 What is a family?

Listen. Say. Sing.

Key Vocabulary: *father, mother, sister, brother*

Tracks: 19 and 20

What is the story about?

Listen. Say. Point.

The Noisy House

duck

lamb

night

Key Vocabulary: *duck, lamb, night, house, small, big, noisy, quiet, family, grandfather, animals, sleep*

Key Language: *What can you see? Who's this? Where does the story take place?*

Track: 21

How does the story help us answer our Big Question?

Listen. Point. Say.

Key Vocabulary: *family, sister, brother, mother, father, grandfather, animal, noisy, quiet, sleep*

Track: 21

Who is in the story?

Look. Say. Color.

Key Vocabulary: *father, mother, grandfather, brother, sister*

Key Language: *Who is in the story?*

Is it important to help our family?

Look. Trace. Talk.

Key Language: *How can we help our family? We can clean. We can help our mother / father.*

Who else is in a family?

Stick. Listen. Say.

Key Vocabulary: *grandfather, grandmother, baby*

Track: 22

Is this a family?

Point. Say. Color.

Key Language: *What is a family? Is this a family? Is he the (father)? Is she the (grandmother)? Yes, s/he is. No, s/he isn't.*

Who is wearing yellow?

Look. Match. Say.

Key Vocabulary: *yellow*

Key Language: *The (paint) is yellow. What color is s/he wearing? The (grandmother) is wearing yellow.*

Tall or short? Young or old?

Match. Listen. Say.

young

old

short

tall

Key Vocabulary: *young, old, short, tall*

Track: 23

What do the family members look like?

Look. Point. Say.

Key Language: *What does s/he look like? S/he's (tall). Is the (sister) old? Yes. / No. My mother is (tall). My brother is (young).*

What are the family members' names?

Say. Listen. Circle.

Key Language: *What's your (mother)'s name? My (mother)'s name is Kim.*

Track: 24

Do animals have families?

Look. Say. Match.

Key Vocabulary: *bear, elephant, penguin, baby animals*

Key Language: *This is the (elephant)'s family.*

How many family members can you see?

Say. Count. Match.

4

Key Vocabulary: *one, two, three, four*

Key Language: *Show me (four). How many (family members) can you see?*

Make. Say.

What is a family?

Key Vocabulary: *mother, father, sister, brother, grandfather, grandmother, baby, young, old, tall, short*
Key Language: *This is my (mother). My (mother)'s name is ...*

5 What is a pet?

Listen. Say. Sing.

dog

bird

rabbit

fish

Key Vocabulary: *dog, bird, rabbit, fish*

Tracks: 25 and 26

What is the story about?

Listen. Point. Say.

Maisie's Pets

cat

run

window

Key Vocabulary: *girl, cat, dog, run, window*

Key Language: *What can you see? What is the story about? Where does it take place?*

Track: 27

How does the story help us answer our Big Question?

Listen. Point. Say.

Key Language: *What can you see? Who are the characters? What is the story about?*

Track: 27

Which scenes are from the story?

Look. Say. Trace.

Key Vocabulary: *character, scene*

Key Language: *Is this a scene from the story? Which scenes are from the story?*

Is it important to take care of our pets?

Look. Trace. Talk.

Key Language: *Take care of our pets. Help our pets. Feed our pets.*

Can you name the pets?

Listen. Say. Trace.

turtle

cat

hamster

lizard

Key Vocabulary: *turtle, cat, hamster, lizard*

Track: 28

Which pet sleeps here?

Stick. Count. Circle.

1 2 3 4

1 2 3 4

1 2 3 4

1 2 3 4

Key Language: *How many (birds) can you see? I can see (two) birds.*

Is the pet big or small?

Point. Say. Match.

Key Vocabulary: *big, small*

Key Language: *Is this (dog) big? Is this (dog) small? Point to a big / small pet.*

Can you name the pets' actions?

Trace. Listen. Say.

walk

jump

swim

fly

Key Vocabulary: *walk, jump, swim, fly*

Track: 29

Can dogs fly?

Point. Say. Color.

Key Language: *Can (cats) walk? Yes, they can. No, they can't. (Cats) can walk. (Cats) can't fly.*

How do pets communicate?

Listen. Point. Say.

Key Language: *Let's pretend. How do (pets) communicate?*

Track: 30

Are all animals pets?

Look. Say. Color.

Key Vocabulary: *wild animals*

Key Language: *What's this? It's a (fish). Is it a pet?*

How many fish can you see?

Say. Count. Trace.

Key Vocabulary: *one, two, three, four, five*

Key Language: *Show me (five). How many (fish) can you see?*

Make. Say.

What is a pet?

1

2

3

4

Key Vocabulary: *dog, bird, rabbit, fish, cat, turtle, hamster, lizard, big, small, fly, walk, jump, swim*
Key Language: *How many (birds) can you see? I can see (three). Can (birds) fly? Yes, they can. No, they can't. Birds can fly. Cats can't fly.*

6 Can healthy foods be delicious?

Listen. Say. Sing.

apple

pear

tomato

carrot

Key Vocabulary: *apple, pear, tomato, carrot*

Tracks: 31 and 32

What is the story about?

Listen. Point. Say.

Healthy Hannah

pear

quail

van

Key Vocabulary: *healthy, pear, quail, van*

Key Language: *What is the story about? What can you see? Who's this? What's this?*

Track: 33

How does the story help us answer our Big Question?

Listen. Point. Say.

Key Vocabulary: *pear, apple, carrot, quail, healthy*

Key Language: *What is the story about? What can you see?*

Track: 33

Which scenes are from the story?

Look. Say. Color.

Key Language: *What is the story about? Who are the characters? Can you remember? Where does the story take place? Is it a scene from the story?*

Is it important to wash fruits and vegetables?

Look. Color. Talk.

Key Language: *Wash fruit and vegetables. Eat healthy food.*

Can you name these healthy foods?

Listen. Say. Color.

bananas

grapes

cucumbers

lettuce

Key Vocabulary: *bananas, grapes, cucumbers, lettuce*

Track: 34

Which foods do you like?

Stick. Say.

Key Language: *Which (foods) do you like? I like (bananas).*

Can you see the circles?

Look. Trace. Say.

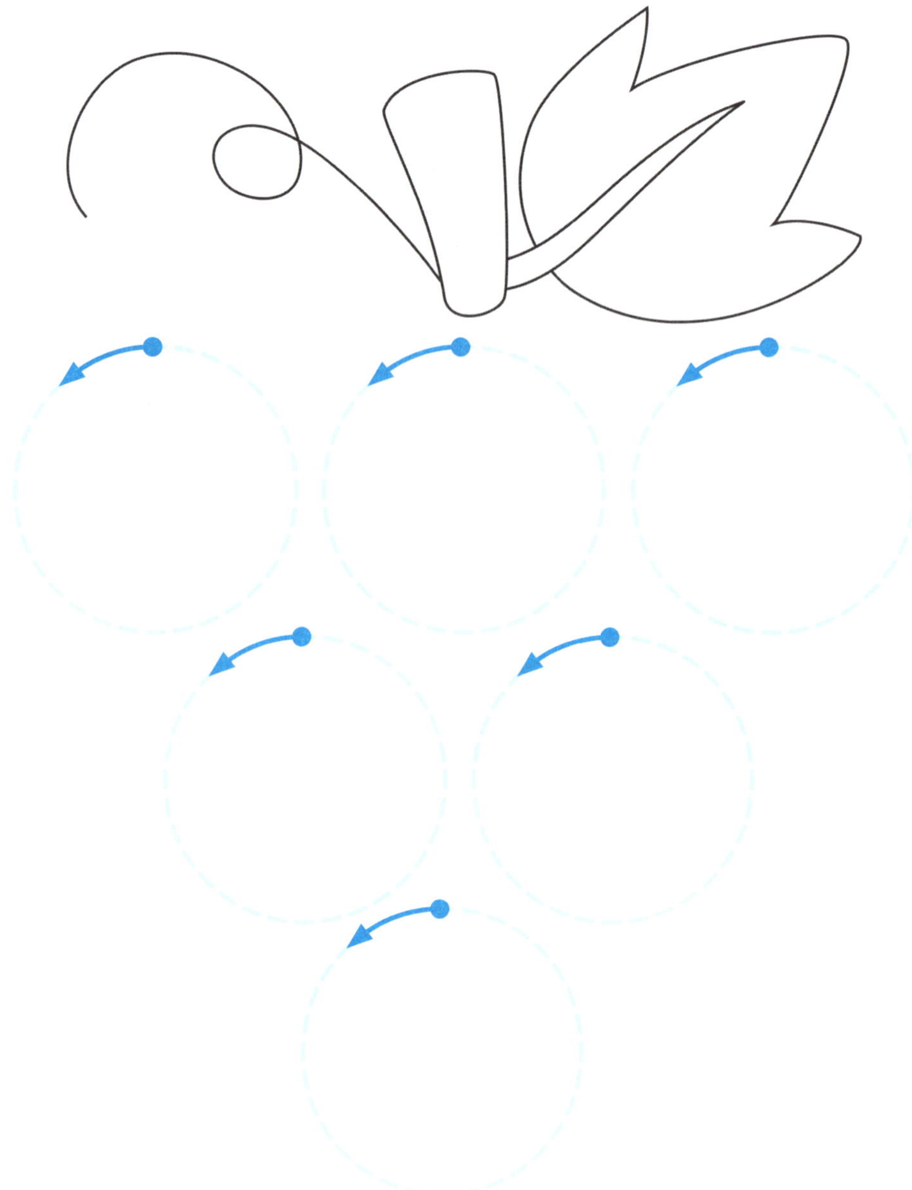

Key Vocabulary: *circle*

Key Language: *What shape is it? Draw circles. Trace the circles.*

Can you find the foods?

Match. Listen. Say.

pineapple

orange

potato

peas

Key Vocabulary: *pineapple, orange, potato, peas*

Track: 35

What do you have in your lunchbox?

Look. Draw. Say.

Key Language: *What does s/he have? S/he has a/an (apple). What do you have? I have a/an (carrot).*

Do you like apples?

Listen. Say. Circle.

Key Language: *Do you like (apples)? Yes, I do. No, I don't. I like (pears). Let's eat …*

Track: 36

What does an apple tree need to grow?

Say. Trace. Color.

Key Language: *What does it need? Does it need (sunlight)? It needs (water).*

How many tomatoes can you see?

Say. Count. Color.

6

Key Vocabulary: *one, two, three, four, five, six*

Key Language: *Show me (six). How many (tomatoes) can you see? Let's count.*

Make. Say.

Can healthy foods be delicious?

1

2

3

4

Key Vocabulary: *apple, pear, tomato, carrot, bananas, grapes, cucumbers, lettuce, pineapple, orange, potato, peas, circle*

Key Language: *What do you like? I like (apples). Do you like (apples)? Yes, I do. No, I don't. It's healthy. I have a/an (apple).*

Track: 32

7 What is a toy?

Listen. Say. Sing.

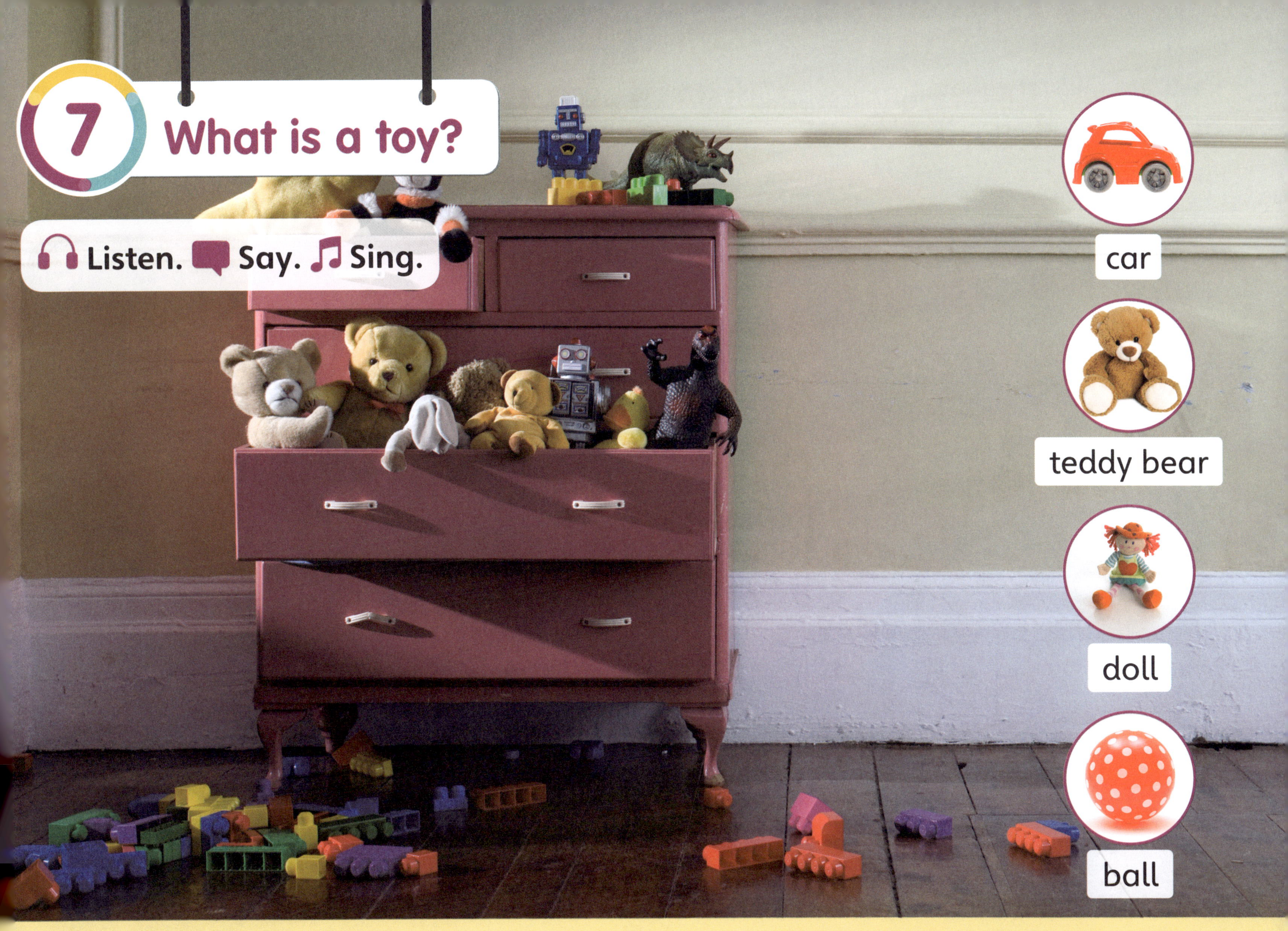

car

teddy bear

doll

ball

Key Vocabulary: *car, teddy bear, doll, ball*

Tracks: 37 and 38

What is the story about?

Listen. Point. Say.

A Little Teddy Bear

yo-yo

zipper

Key Vocabulary: *yo-yo, zipper, teddy bear, toy*

Key Language: *What can you see? What is the story about? Who's this?*

Track: 39

How does the story help us answer our Big Question?

Listen. Point. Say.

Key Vocabulary: *teddy bear, toy*

Key Language: *What can you see? What is the story about? Who's this?*

Track: 39

What does Teddy do next?

Look. Say. Stick.

Key Language: *What does Teddy do first / next?*

Is it important to share our toys?

Look. Trace. Talk.

Key Vocabulary: *share*

Key Language: *Who is sharing?*

Can you match the toys?

Listen. Say. Match.

kite

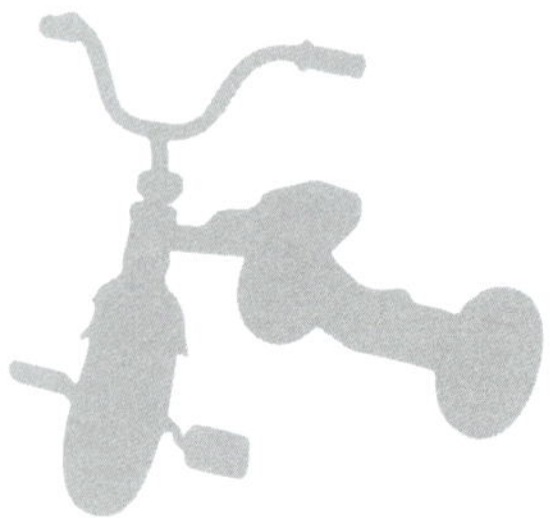

tricycle

blocks

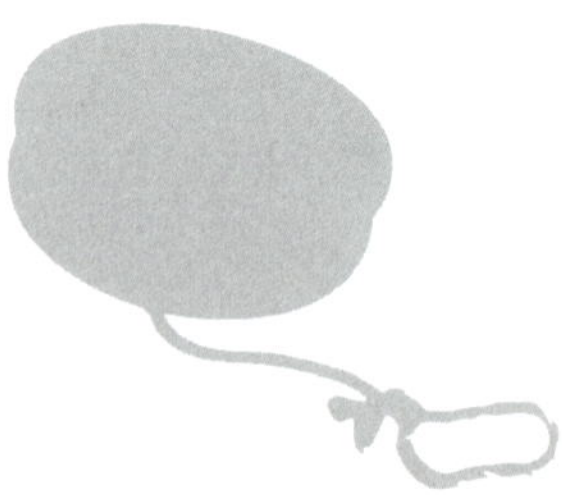

yo-yo

Key Vocabulary: *kite, tricycle, blocks, yo-yo*

What color is the toy?

Look. Say. Color.

Key Language: *What color is the (ball)? The (ball) is (red). It's (red).*

Can you find the squares?

Look. Say. Color.

Key Language: *What shape is it? It's a square.*

What toy is it?

Listen. Point. Say.

train

puzzle

board game

robot

Key Vocabulary: *train, puzzle, board game, robot*

Track: 41

Is it small? Is it blue?

Point. Circle. Say.

Key Vocabulary: *big, small, red, blue, yellow, ball, car, robot*

Key Language: *Is it (big)? Is it (red)? Yes, it is. No, it isn't. The (ball) is (small) and (blue).*

Which toy do you want?

Listen. Say. Trace.

Key Language: *I want a (teddy bear), please. Here you are. Thank you.*

Tracks: 38 and 42

Can you match the toys?

Look. Match.

Key Vocabulary: *teddy bear, doll, robot*

How many toys can you see?

Say. Count. Color.

7

Key Vocabulary: *one, two, three, four, five, six, seven*

Key Language: *Let's count. Show me (seven). How many (toys) can you see?*

Make. Say.

What is a toy?

1

2

3

4

Key Vocabulary: *toys, teddy bear, doll, ball, car, yo-yo, kite, tricycle, blocks, puzzle, board game, train, robot*

Key Language: *What color is the (ball)? It's (blue). Is it (small)? Yes, it is. No, it isn't. The ball is small and blue.*

8 What can we see in a park?

Listen. Say. Sing.

tree

flower

grass

bee

Key Vocabulary: *tree, flower, grass, bee*

Tracks: 43 and 44

What is the story about?

Listen. Point. Say.

Let's Play Together!

ant

iguana

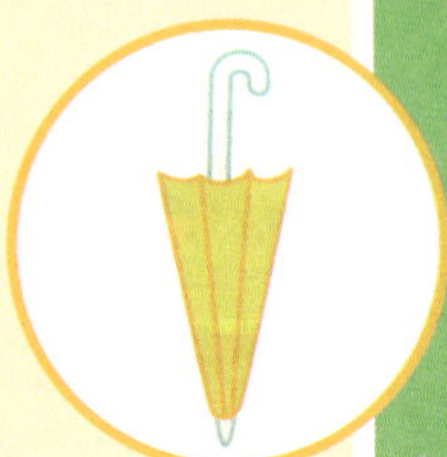

umbrella

Key Vocabulary: *ant, iguana, umbrella*

Key Language: *Where is (my teddy bear)? It's (on) the swing.*

Track: 45

How does the story help us answer our Big Question?

Listen. Point. Say.

Key Language: *Where is the (iguana)? Why do they need (an umbrella)?*

Track: 45

What happens first, next, and last?

Say. Color.

Key Language: *What happens first / next / last?*

Is it important to keep parks clean?

Look. Trace. Talk.

Key Vocabulary: *park, clean*

Can you name the objects in the park?

Listen. Say. Color.

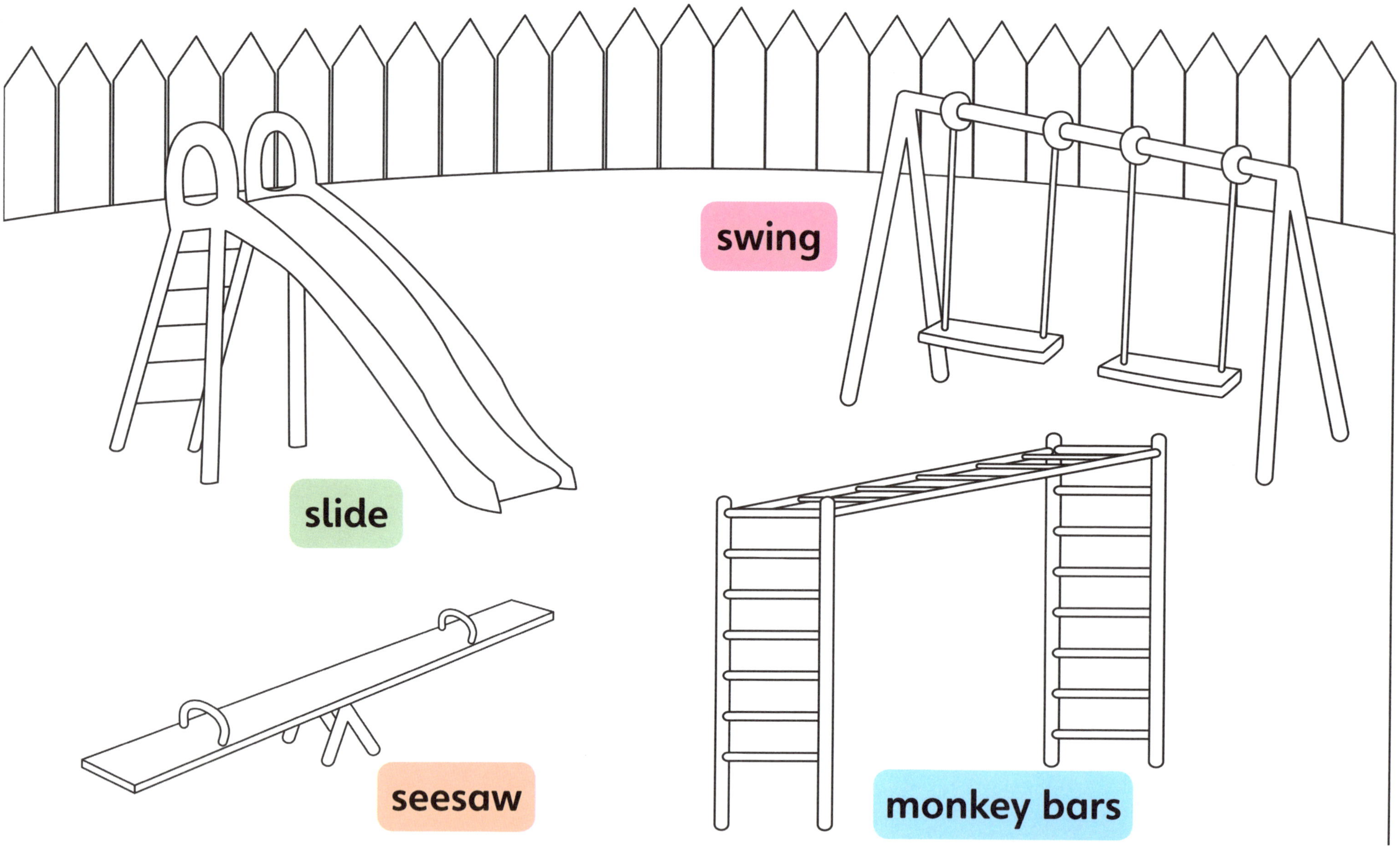

Key Vocabulary: *slide, swing, seesaw, monkey bars*

Track: 46

Do you like to play in the park?

Say. Stick.

Key Vocabulary: *slide, swing, seesaw, monkey bars*

Key Language: *Do you like to play on the (swings)? Yes, I do. No, I don't.*

Can you find the triangles?

Look. Point. Color.

Key Vocabulary: *triangle, circle, square*

Key Language: *What shape is it? It's a triangle.*

What else can we see in a park?

Match. Listen. Say.

sun

cloud

sky

butterfly

Key Vocabulary: *sun, cloud, sky, butterfly*

Track: 47

What's wrong?

Look. Draw. Say.

Key Language: *What can you see? I can see a butterfly / some clouds.*

What does a tree look like?

Listen. Say. Color.

Key Vocabulary: *big, small, red, yellow, blue, green*

Key Language: *What color is it? (It's red.) What does a (tree) look like? It's (big).*

Track: 48

What can you see in a park?

Say. Color.

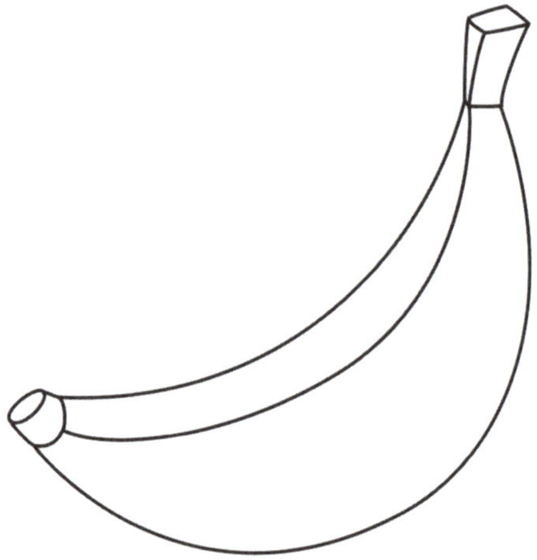

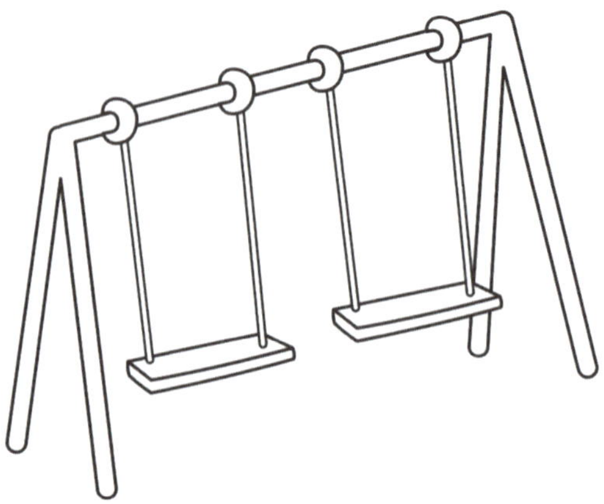

Key Language: *What can you see in a park? Can you see a ...? Yes. No.*

How many flowers can you see?

Say. Count. Color.

8

Key Vocabulary: *one, two, three, four, five, six, seven, eight*

Key Language: *Let's count. Show me (eight). How many (flowers) can you see?*

Make. Say.

What can we see in a park?

1

2

3

4

Key Vocabulary: *tree, flower, bee, grass, slide, swing, seesaw, monkey bars, sun, cloud, sky, butterfly, green, red, blue, yellow, big, small*
Key Language: *What can you see at the park? I can see a seesaw / some trees. Do you like to play on the (swings)? Yes, I do. No, I don't.*

9 Where do we live?

Listen. Say. Sing.

city

country

house

farm

Key Vocabulary: *city, country, house, farm*

Tracks: 49 and 50

What is the story about?

Listen. Point. Say.

There Is a Woman Who Lives in an Orange Shoe

elephant

orange

Key Vocbaulary: *orange, elephant, children*

Key Language: *Who lives in a shoe? Where does she live?*

Track: 51

How does the story help us answer our Big Question?

Listen. Point. Say.

Key Language: *What can you see? What is the story about? Where are they?*

Track: 51

What happens first, next, and last?

Look. Say. Stick.

1

2

3

Key Language: *What happens first / next / last?*

How can you show you love someone?

Look. Say. Color.

Key Vocabulary: *love, mother, father, grandmother, grandfather*

What is it?

Listen. Say. Trace.

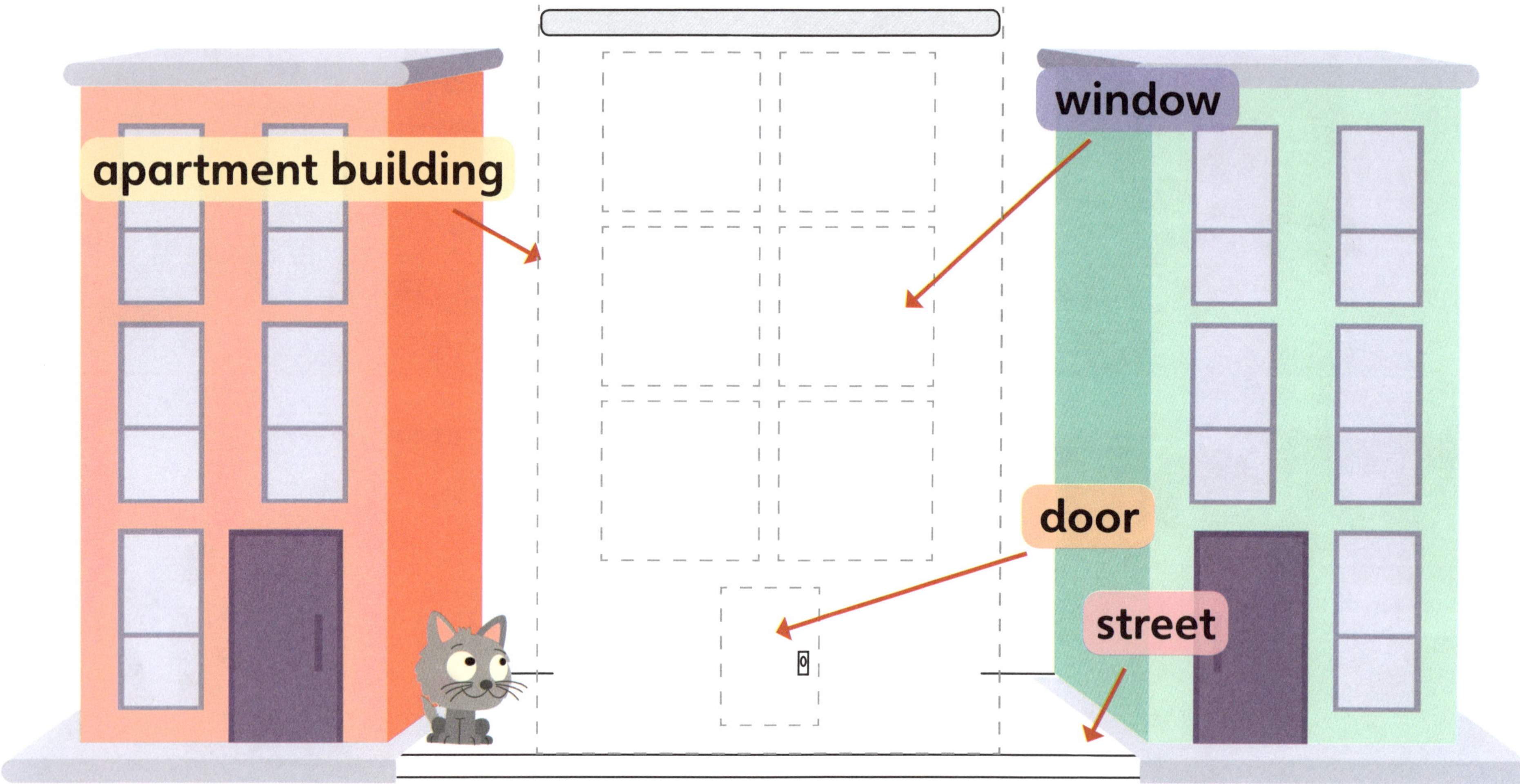

Key Vocabulary: *apartment building, window, door, street*

Track: 52

Where do they live?

Follow. Color. Say.

Key Vocabulary: *house, apartment building*

Key Language: *Where does s/he live? S/he lives in (a house). Where do you live? I live in (an apartment building).*

Is the house near or far?

Say. Follow. Color.

Key Vocabulary: *near, far*

Key Language: *The (park) is near. The (house) is far.*

Where can you see these objects?

Listen. Say. Match.

market

toy store

park

playground

Key Vocabulary: *tree, swing, apple, yo-yo, market, toy store, park, playground*

Track: 53

What can you see near your house?

Draw. Match. Say.

Key Vocabulary: *school, street, park, market, playground*

Key Language: *What can you see near your house? (A park.)*

Where can they go?

Listen. Match. Say.

Key Vocabulary: *run, want, buy, toy store, park*

Key Language: *I want to (run). Let's go to the (park)!*

Track: 54

What can we see in the city and in the country?

Look. Say. Circle.

Key Vocabulary: *country, city, apartment building, bus, horse, park, sheep, toy store*

Key Language: *Can you see a (bus) in the (country)? I can see a (toy store) in the city.*

How many windows can you see?

Say. 1 2 3 Count. Color.

9

10

Key Vocabulary: *one, two, three, four, five, six, seven, eight, nine, ten*

Key Language: *Let's count. How many (windows) can you see?*

Track: 50

Make. Say.

Where do we live?

1

2

3

4

Key Vocabulary: *house, city, country, farm, street, apartment building, door, window, park, market, playground, toy store*

Key Language: *I live in (a house). I can see a (park) near my house.*

Fall Tree

Paint. Cut. Make.

Ask: *What happens to the leaves in fall?* Provide any necessary language. Then children dip the tips of their fingers in orange, yellow, and brown finger paint and apply their fingerprints to the tree. Allow the paint to dry. Then they cut the picture as shown and mix up the pieces. Finally, children put the puzzle together.

Winter Bear

Cut. Glue. Make.

Ask: *What's the weather like in winter?* Provide any necessary language. Help children cut out the bear, the scarf and the hat. Children glue the bear's head onto a piece of white paper and draw the bear's body. Provide small squares of white tissue paper. Children scrunch up the paper and glue it onto the bear's head and body. Finally, they cut out the hat and scarf and glue them on the bear.

Spring Chick and Bird

Cut. Glue. Make.

Ask: *What's the weather like in spring?* Provide any necessary language. Help children cut out the pictures. Then they glue feathers onto the chick and the bird. Children put their fingers into the two holes and play with their puppets.

Summer Popsicle

Cut. Glue. Make.

Ask: *What's the weather like in summer?* Provide any necessary language. Children cut out the two popsicles, glue them onto construction paper paper and cut them out again. Children glue buttons, stickers, and / or cereal on the popsicles to decorate them. Finally, they glue a wooden stick to the back of the popsicles.

Unit 1, p. 9

Unit 3, p. 36

Unit 4, p. 50

Unit 5, p. 65

Unit 6, p. 79

Unit 7, p. 90

Unit 8, p. 107

Unit 9, p. 118